Follow Me Around™
Japan

By Wiley Blevins

■ SCHOLASTIC

Content Consultant: Hiroko C. Kataoka, PhD, Professor of Japanese, Department of Asian and Asian American Studies, California State University, Long Beach, California

Library of Congress Cataloging-in-Publication Data
Names: Blevins, Wiley, author.
Title: Japan / by Wiley Blevins.
Description: New York : Children's Press, an imprint of Scholastic Inc., 2018. |
Series: Follow me around | Includes bibliographical references and index.
Identifiers: LCCN 2016050907| ISBN 9780531237052 (library binding : alk. paper) | ISBN 9780531239711 (pbk. : alk. paper)
Subjects: LCSH: Japan—Juvenile literature.
Classification: LCC DS806 .B525 2018 | DDC 952—dc23
LC record available at https://lccn.loc.gov/2016050907

Design: Judith Christ Lafond & Anna Tunick Tabachnik
Text: Wiley Blevins
© 2018 Scholastic Inc.

Photographs ©: cover girl: The International Photo Co./Getty Images; cover main: Sean Pavone/Dreamstime; back cover: The International Photo Co./Getty Images; 1: The International Photo Co./Getty Images; 3: Jose Fuste Raga/Getty Images; 4 left: The International Photo Co./Getty Images; 6: JohnnyGreig/iStockphoto; 7 left: MIXA next/Thinkstock; 7 right: Skye Hohmann/Alamy Images; 8 top: Hideo Haga/HAGA/The Image Works; 8 center top: PRASAN MAKSAEN/Shutterstock; 8 bottom: Bajnoci Peter/Shutterstock; 8 center bottom: ALLEKO/iStockphoto; 9 top: Prostock-studio/Shutterstock; 9 bottom right: oluolu3/iStockphoto; 9 bottom left: Y_L/Shutterstock; 10 left: imtmphoto/Shutterstock; 10 top right: recep-bg/iStockphoto; 10 bottom right: taketan/Getty Images; 11: Futaba Hayashi/Dreamstime; 12 frogs: Afanasia/Shutterstock; 12-13 background: Vadim Yerofeyev/Dreamstime; 13 top: benntennsann/Shutterstock; 13 bottom: PinkPeng/Shutterstock; 14 top: AlpamayoPhoto/iStockphoto; 14 bottom: NicolasMcComber/iStockphoto; 15 right: Nikada/iStockphoto; 15 center: Leonid Andronov/iStockphoto; 15 left: Marco Ciannarella/Dreamstime; 16 left: Lucas Vallecillos/age fotostock; 16 right: Nikada/iStockphoto; 17 bottom right: jiratto/Shutterstock; 17 left: Marco Ciannarella/Dreamstime; 17 top right: Prisma by Dukas Presseagentur GmbH/Alamy Images; 18 left: Werner Forman/Universal Images Group/Getty Images; 18 right: World History Archive/Alamy Images; 19 top: Andrew Melbourne/Alamy Images; 19 bottom left: Universal Images Group North America LLC/Alamy Images; 19 bottom center: Bettmann/Getty Images; 19 bottom right: f11photo/Shutterstock; 20 top: Jose Fuste Raga/Getty Images; 20 center: UnlistedImages/Media Bakery; 20 bottom: YOSHIKAZU TSUNO/AFP/Getty Images; 21 top: Lucas Vallecillos/age fotostock/Superstock, Inc.; 21 bottom left: age fotostock/Superstock, Inc.; 21 bottom right: KPG Payless2/Shutterstock; 22: baoyan/Shutterstock; 23 top right: JTB Photo/Superstock, Inc.; 23 center top left: MichikoDesign/iStockphoto; 23 center bottom left: ziggy_mars/iStockphoto; 23 bottom left: Sankei/Getty Images; 23 top right: karins/Shutterstock; 24 left: kokouu/iStockphoto; 24 right: tofang/Shutterstock; 25 left: mauritius images GmbH/Alamy Images; 25 right: Lucas Vallecillos/V&W/The Image Works; 26: JohnnyGreig/iStockphoto; 27 top left: agcuesta/iStockphoto; 27 bottom left: koi88/Shutterstock; 27 bottom right: OGphoto/iStockphoto; 27 top right: coward_lion/iStockphoto; 28 A.: Patrick_Gijsbers/iStockphoto; 28 B.: pnphotos/iStockphoto; 28 C.: Abbie Enock/age fotostock; 28 D.: SeanPavonePhoto/iStockphoto; 28 E.: prasit_chansareekorn/iStockphoto; 28 F.: JuliaWimmerlin/iStockphoto; 28 G.: TommL/iStockphoto; 30 top right: EPS10J/Shutterstock; 30 top left: marigold_88/iStockphoto; 30 bottom: The International Photo Co./Getty Images. Maps by Jim McMahon.

Table of Contents

Where in the World Is Japan?

Konnichiwa (kohn-nee-chee-wah) from Japan! That's how we say "hello." I'm Satchiko (saht-chee-koh), your tour guide. My name means "lucky child." And it's true—I am lucky! I was lucky to be chosen to show you around my island country.

Japan is in Asia and is made up of more than 6,000 islands. It's about the same size as the state of California. We live on what is called the Ring of Fire. It is an area that has a lot of earthquakes and volcanoes. But we also have some of the best hot springs around!

Fast Facts:

- **The four main islands of Japan are Honshu (the biggest), Hokkaido, Shikoku, and Kyushu. The country is about 1,864 miles (3,000 kilometers) from north to south.**

- **Approximately 70 percent of Japan is covered by mountains.**

- **Mount Fuji is the tallest mountain in the country.**

- **The Pacific Ocean lies to the east of Japan. To the west you'll find the Sea of Japan, the Korea Strait, and the East China Sea.**

CHINA

RUSSIA

Sapporo

HOKKAIDO

NORTH
KOREA

Sea of Japan
(East Sea)

JAPAN

Sendai

HONSHU

SOUTH
KOREA

Yellow
Sea

Korea
Strait

Hiroshima

Osaka

Mount
Fuji

Tokyo

PACIFIC
OCEAN

Fukuoka

SHIKOKU

East
China
Sea

KYUSHU

OKINAWA

Phillipine
Sea

5

Some Japanese homes use low tables. However, Western-style tables and chairs are also common.

Home Sweet Home

I am from Tokyo, Japan. I live with my parents and little brother in a unit that is part of a tall building with many other units. In Japan, we call where we live a *manshon*. You might call it an apartment or a condo. Most apartments in my city are small and simply decorated. Most of our furniture is probably pretty familiar, such as tables, chairs, desks, and beds. In winter, some people use a special low table called a *kotatsu*. This table is heated and covered with a special blanket so it keeps us nice and warm!

If you visit my home, the first thing you do is take off your shoes. We never wear shoes indoors. Inside, we put on slippers. We have special slippers for the kitchen and bathroom. Wear your favorite socks, and make sure they don't have any holes!

Kitchen

Our kitchen has two **essentials**: a rice cooker and an electric tea kettle. There is also a microwave, a toaster oven, and a stovetop.

Our bathrooms are high tech. They often have heated floors. We can also set our bathtub water to an exact temperature! Toilets are usually in a separate room. They have heated seats and multiple flushing options that help **conserve** water.

Bathing in Japan

Japanese bath

1 **Outside the tub,** pour water over your head and body with a small bucket. The water runs down a drain at your feet.

2 Next, **soap up** and shampoo.

3 **Rinse off** by pouring more water over your head.

4 **Soak** in the tub filled with hot water for 10 minutes.

5 **Get out and dry off.** Now you're squeaky clean!

6 **Place the bathtub cover** over the tub and leave it ready for the next person. We share bathwater with our family.

Let's Eat

Before eating, we say "itadakimasu" (ee-tah-dah-kee-mahs), which means "I humbly receive this food."

Since Japan is surrounded by water, we eat a lot of seafood. We also eat a lot of noodle, bread, and rice dishes. Throughout most of our country's history, people ate rice at every meal. So the word for "meal," *gohan*, is the same as the word for "cooked rice."

Meals are based around rice, noodles, or sometimes bread, plus a meat dish with vegetables. Fish and seafood can be eaten raw (**sushi** or sashimi), sun-dried and grilled, fried, or broiled. On

Rice

Miso soup

Bento box

the side, you'll be served seasonal vegetables such as radishes, onions, cabbage, and carrots. You'll also be served soup, which you drink from the bowl. Slurp! Miso soup is really popular. Miso is a salty paste made from soybeans, and it's very yummy. At the end of the meal, we like to eat pickles. Many different vegetables are pickled. They come in a variety of flavors—salt, sugar, vinegar, citrus, and herbs. An entire meal to go for one person can be packed in a bento box.

Sushi

Forget about forks and knives when eating in Japan. We eat with chopsticks. You might want to practice before you come. Here's how:

1 Place the thick end of a chopstick in the crook of your thumb.

2 Let the chopstick rest on your ring finger.

3 Place the other chopstick between the tips of your first two fingers and the tip of your thumb.

4 To grab food, move the top chopstick up and down.

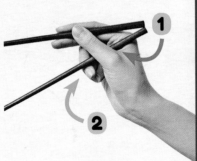

Tea Ceremony

Tea is important in Japan. The tea ceremony is a formal and elegant way for a small group of people to make and serve tea. It has been done in Japan since the 16th century and is one of our most treasured **traditions**. The host wears a kimono, uses a powdered green tea, and follows a set of steps and movements to make, serve, and drink the tea. The ceremony can last up to four hours.

Tea ceremony

Students in uniform

Cleaning the school

We are responsible for cleaning our classroom. It's a daily chore we all share.

Cherry blossoms

Off to School

In Japan, we start school in April. It's also when the *sakura*, or cherry blossoms, bloom. It's a special time of beginnings for us. Our school week is five days long, the same as it is in the United States, but our school day is longer. After school, many students go to a *juku*, or cram school. A cram school is a private school that helps us prepare for big tests. There, the classes are smaller. My school also has extra activities on some Saturdays. Our summer vacation lasts a little more than a month. As you can see, that's a lot of school!

One of the first things we learn in school is how to read and write. Writing is considered an art form. We learn how to write in special classes called *shodō*.

There are three types of writing in Japanese. *Kanji* is a set of characters that stand for words. There are about 2,000 kanji in use today. *Hiragana* is a little simpler. It has only 46 characters that stand for 46 sounds. Women developed it 1,000 years ago. The third type of writing is *Katakana*. It is a set of characters used to write foreign words—like your name! We also learn the English letters, called *Rōmaji*.

In some sentences, multiple types of writing are used at the same time. Below, the blue text is Kanji, red is Hiragana, orange is Katakana, and green is Rōmaji. The sentence translates to, "Please send me that photo as a jpeg file."

その写真をjpegファイルで送ってください。

(Sono shashin o jpeg fairu de okutte kudasai.)

Counting to 10 is important to know when you visit Japan. We often use the same numerals as in the United States (such as 1, 2, and 3). We can also, however, write numbers using the kanji characters below.

一	1	**ichi** *(ee-chee)*
二	2	**ni** *(nee)*
三	3	**san** *(sahn)*
四	4	**shi** *(shee)*
五	5	**go** *(goh)*
六	6	**roku** *(roh-koo)*
七	7	**shichi** *(shee-chee)*
八	8	**hachi** *(hah-chee)*
九	9	**kyu-u** *(kyoo-oo)*
十	10	**jyu-u** *(jyoo-oo)*

Haiku

In school, we learn to write haiku. These are special three-line poems. They follow a specific pattern based on the number of syllables in each line. A haiku can be about anything, but many are about nature or the seasons. Some haiku are serious. Some are descriptive. Others are really funny.

Rules for Writing a Haiku

1 The first line has 5 syllables.

2 The second line has 7 syllables.

3 The third line has 5 syllables.

4 Traditional haikus have a word that shows a season, such as "frog" for spring and "hot" for summer. Modern haikus, however, do not always include a season word.

An old silent pond . . .
A frog jumps into the pond,
splash! Silence again.
—Matsuo Basho

I walk across sand
And find myself blistering
In the hot, hot heat.

My favorite book
Dragons, castles, and a prince
Who will rule the land?

Little brothers, ugh
Mom says he has to stay but
I say why not vote?

13

Tokyo

Touring Japan

Tokyo: Capital City

Welcome to my city, Tokyo. It's the capital of Japan. More than 13 million people live here. In fact, more than three-fourths of all Japanese live in cities such as Tokyo. When you come here, you'll want to go first to the Tokyo Skytree, an observation tower. Visit the deck and look out over my huge city. There is even a glass floor in some parts. If you're afraid of heights, don't look down!

Your next stop might be at an *onsen*, or natural hot spring. There are a few special ones for visitors. Men and women are separated, so bring a family member or friend who can stick with you. Rinse off, hop in, and relax. Just one warning: no clothes allowed.

Onsen

Hachikō statue

Imperial Palace

Shibuya Crossing

Did you ever think a street crossing could be fun? Go to the Shibuya Crossing, wait for the light, and then cross this wide street as fast as you can. More than a thousand others will try to cross at the same time going every direction. They don't call it "the scramble" for nothing. A giant video screen and flashing neon lights make this a once-in-a-lifetime experience.

The Imperial Palace is also a must-see. This castle still houses the current **emperor** of Japan, so you can't go inside. You can walk the surrounding gardens. It's like stepping back in time.

My last favorite stop is at the statue of Hachikō. He's the most famous dog in Japan. He used to greet his owner at the Shibuya Station (a train station) every day when he returned from work. After his owner died, he continued to go to the station in hopes his owner would return one day. Hachikō did this for 10 more years. A movie was made about his life. The statue was created in memory of this remarkable dog's loyalty.

Whale shark mascot

Osaka Aquarium

Dotonbori

Osaka

Travel southwest of Tokyo and visit the city of Osaka. It has more than 2.7 million people. Your first stop should be the Osaka Aquarium, known as Kaiyukan. It's the biggest aquarium in the world. Be on the lookout for the whale shark, the aquarium's **mascot**.

You might also check out Dotonbori. It's a popular shopping street. The giant animated food signs make it even more fun. Look up and you'll spot moving crabs, octopuses, and dragons. One of the special foods there is *okonomiyaki*. That's a tasty pancake with cabbage and meat, topped with red pickled ginger, bonito flakes (a bonito is a type of fish), and a special sauce. Another special food is *takoyaki*. These are small dough balls with pieces of octopus. Yum!

Golden Pavilion

Buddha at the Todaiji Temple

Mount Fuji

Bullet train

Other Fun Places

Hop on the bullet train, called *shinkansen* (sheen-kahn-sehn), and go to Kyoto. This historical city is important for traditional Japanese arts and religion. It has a lot of **shrines** and temples. Your first stop should be Kiyomizudera. It's a famous temple on a hill overlooking the area. It's a great climb for tourists, and you can buy fun **souvenirs** on the way up.

Another must-see is Kinkakuji, or the Golden Pavilion. The shiny temple is one of the most beautiful sites you'll ever see. When the leaves turn colors in autumn or bloom in the spring, it's packed with people.

Since you're close, visit the nearby city of Nara. The Todaiji Temple there is famous. It is the largest wooden building in the world, and it is home to a massive and beautiful bronze Buddha.

Our Fascinating History

We're proud of our country's long history. Today, Japan is truly a globalized society. We openly trade art, ideas, and products with people around the world. For more than a thousand years, however, our rulers controlled our contact with other countries, such as China and Korea. This was so we could learn from their cultures but also stay independent.

Haniwa

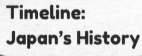

Samurai

Timeline: Japan's History

2500 BCE
Pre-history
People first begin to grow rice. Large burial mounds are built. Their contents include clay figures called *haniwa*.

about 7th Century CE
The Age of Nobility
People begin building large cities. *Kana*, a form of Japanese writing, is invented.

about 1100s to 1800s
The Age of Warriors
Samurai warriors fight for their feudal lords. They report to the shogun, or general of the emperor's army. The shogun had the true power (even over the emperor). Great castles are built.

You can still visit many places in Japan that are like stepping back in time. You'll see ancient temples, former samurai districs, and geisha with their white painted faces and beautiful **kimonos**.

Geisha

Kabuki actor

1600s-1800s

The Age of the Merchants

More people move to cities. Merchants grow in wealth and power. Kabuki, a type of theater, becomes popular.

mid-1800s

The Age of Opening to the World

Japan opens trade with other countries. An emperor rules the country. The city of Edo is renamed Tokyo.

Today

Japan Today
Japan is a world power.

It Came From Japan

A kimono is a traditional Japanese dress. Both men and women wear it. Today we only wear kimonos for special occasions, such as weddings, some holidays, and tea ceremonies.

Everywhere in Japan you'll hear people singing karaoke. The word *karaoke* means "empty orchestra" in Japanese. Just listen to the music and follow along to the words on the screen.

A lot of our most popular music is idol pop by groups such as AKB48 or solo artists like Kyary Pamyu Pamyu. Idol pop stars are usually young and have crowds of devoted fans.

Manga are hugely popular comics created using a special style of art developed in Japan. My friends and I love to buy, borrow, trade, or rent them. There are also manga festivals that are a lot of fun. People dress up as their favorite characters. Some people also bring homemade comics to share or sell.

Anime is a style of animated films also developed in Japan. Most characters have oversized eyes and often colorful hair in unique styles. You might have seen anime such as the Pokémon films.

Ninjas, or *shinobi*, are other popular characters in Japanese movies. Long ago, ninjas were highly trained, skilled spies. The ninjas of the past wore navy blue at night. During the day, they dressed to blend in with the people around them.

21

Celebrate!

Everyone loves a holiday. Shōgatsu is the most important in Japan and my favorite holiday. It is our New Year celebration. The temple bells are struck 108 times to go from the old year to the new one.

The most important part of the New Year holiday is called *mochi-tsuki*. This takes place a few days before New Year's Day. Special sticky rice is pounded and shaped into slightly flattened balls called *mochi*. These rice cakes are offered to the gods. We eat smaller ones at our New Year's meal.

Most people travel to be with their families for the celebration. People also send *nenga-jō*, or special greeting postcards, to family and friends. Many are homemade and show the *eto*, or zodiac animal, for the year.

In Which Year Were You Born?

Horse	2002, 2014
Sheep	2003, 2015
Monkey	2004, 2016
Rooster	2005, 2017
Dog	2006, 2018
Boar	2007, 2019
Rat	2008, 2020
Ox	2009, 2021
Tiger	2010, 2022
Hare	2011, 2023
Dragon	2012, 2024
Snake	2013, 2025

February

Sapporo Snow Festival (Yuki-Matsuri)
Huge snow sculptures draw large crowds to this winter festival.

May

Children's Day (Kodomo-No-Hi)
This is celebrated on the fifth day of the fifth month. It used to be called Boy's Day. Brightly colored cloth carp—a fish known for its courage—are flown from tall bamboo poles.

March

Doll Festival or Girl's Day (Hina-Matsuri)
This is celebrated on the third day of the third month. Many girls display their dolls.

August

Festival of the Souls (O-Bon)
People welcome back the spirits of their **ancestors**. A fire is lit. People put fruit, vegetables, rice, and flowers on family altars.

Make Onigiri Rice Balls

Ingredients:
Rice, *nori* (thin, flat sheets of seaweed), salt, filling of your choice (grilled and flaked salted salmon is close to traditional *onigiri*)

Ask an adult to help!

Directions:

1 **Cook the rice** and put it in a large bowl to cool slightly. Add salt (about ½ teaspoon for every 3 cups of cooked rice).

2 **Wet your hands.** Then shape ½ cup of rice into a ball. Continue making rice balls until all the rice is used.

3 **Make a depression** (indent) in the center of a rice ball with your thumb.

4 **Put the filling** in the depression. Then press or mold the rice ball so it covers all the filling.

5 **Place a piece** of nori around the rice ball. Squeeze a bit so it sticks.

6 **Do the same** for each of the remaining rice balls.

Eat and enjoy!

23

Origami paper crane

Time to Play

Origami is an art form nearly every kid in Japan learns. No glue or scissors are needed—only paper! This folded-paper art started in Japan in the 1600s.

The Japanese paper crane is the most common and popular figure we make. It symbolizes peace and hope for many people, including a young girl named Sadako Sasaki. She developed cancer after her home in Hiroshima was bombed during World War II. She folded more than 1,000 paper cranes while in the hospital before she died in 1955.

Origami Dog

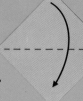

Let's make an origami dog. Follow the steps below. You'll just need a square piece of paper.

Directions:

1. Lay the square paper like a diamond. Fold the top corner to the bottom corner. This will make a triangle.

2. Fold the triangle in half, moving the left corner to the right corner. Press down to make a crease. Then unfold it back to the larger triangle shape.

3. Make the dog's ears. Fold the left and right corners of the triangle down so the tips point down.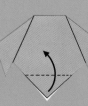

4. Separate the two pieces of paper at the bottom corner, which form the dog's pointy chin. Fold one piece forward.

5. Fold the other corner piece to the back.

6. Draw a cute face on your dog. Ruff! Ruff!

Indoor ski slope

Sumo wrestlers

Sports are a popular pastime in Japan. Soccer is the most popular sport. Basketball and baseball are also favorites. Japan is filled with mountains, so skiing is common. Some cities even have indoor ski slopes. Many people love to swim and dance, too, which we learn in school.

Every autumn, we have the **Annual** Sports Day at school. We compete in races, gymnastics, and tug-of-war. It lasts all day, and our families come to cheer us on.

In Japan, we also have some special sports, including sumo wrestling and many kinds of martial arts (judo, karate-do, kendo, and aikido). Sumo wrestling is Japan's national sport and is more than 1,000 years old. Sumo matches regularly appear on TV. Two wrestlers meet inside a ring, or circle. Their goal is to push the other outside it or knock the opponent down. Sumo wrestlers eat a lot so they are as big as possible. I mean *really* big!

You Won't Believe This!

Taking a bow is very important in Japan. It is how we show respect to others. The higher a person's status, the lower the bow. We bow to our teacher at the beginning and end of school lessons. We bow to signal the end of a conversation. We also bow when we say "please" and "thank you." Talk about polite!

How to Bow

1   Stand straight. Make eye contact.

2   Bend forward at the waist. Look down. If you are a boy, place your hands at your sides. If you're a girl, hold your hands together in front of your thighs.

3   Say something, such as "Thank you." Straighten up and make eye contact.

Here are some things you can say when bowing. Practice them before visiting Japan.

onegai shimasu (oh-nay-gye shee-mahs)—please (when making a request)

arigatō gozaimasu (ah-ree-gah-toh goh-zye-mahs)—thank you

sayōnara (sah-yoh-na-ra)—good-bye

ohayō gozaimasu (o-hah-yoh goh-zye-mahs)—good morning

You'll see statues of cute cats waving one paw all over Japan. These little statues, called *maneki neko*, are for good luck. They are common in stores and restaurants. If the cat's right paw is raised, it invites money into the business. A raised left paw invites in people.

You can get lots of fun things from vending machines in Japan. Funny socks. Pumpkin soup. Even ramen noodles with a tiny spoon. Put in some yen, or money, and pick your favorite.

Some people love nature. One way to reflect that love at home is through *bonsai*. Bonsai are plantings of tiny trees in containers. It's a special Japanese art form.

Japanese calligraphy, or *shodoō*, is a special and beautiful form of writing. Calligraphers use a brush and ink to form the characters. Shodoō is often used to create beautiful works of art on rice paper, or added to objects as decaration.

Guessing Game!

Here are some other great sites around Japan. Can you guess which is which?

Visit this park, a memorial to the site where one of two atomic bombs was dropped during World War II.
G

This is the most active volcano in Japan.
A

1. Arashiyama Bamboo Grove
2. Beppu
3. Hiroshima Peace Memorial
4. Jihokudani Monkey Park
5. Mount Aso
6. Mount Fuji
7. Toei Kyoto Studio Park

These monkeys love to bathe in the hot springs here.
F

This place is famous for its hot springs. Hop in and enjoy!
B

This is the highest mountain in Japan. The bullet train speeds by it.
E

This bamboo grove is one of the most photographed places in the world.
D

Here you can dress up as a samurai warrior, ninja, or geisha and travel back in time.
C

28

Preparing for Your Visit

By now you should be ready to hop on a plane to Japan. Here are some tips to prepare for your trip around my country.

1 Before you come to Japan, exchange your money. Our money is called yen. You'll need it to buy fun souvenirs.

2 If you have some extra money to spend on travel, take the Narita Express from the airport into Tokyo. This train is an exciting way to get into the city. Our trains are super clean and always on time. At each train station, you can get a special stamp, called *eki sutanpu*. Collect them all to remember the stations on your trip!

3 If you're short on money and a bit hungry, stop in a *konbini*, or convenience store. Most are open 24 hours. You can get great food, such as stuffed rice balls, stew, bento boxes, sandwiches, salads, instant ramen noodles, yogurt, and more.

4 You can also go with your family to a *kaitenzushi* restaurant for a less expensive meal. The sushi rolls by on a conveyor belt. Just grab and gobble.

5 If there's an emergency and you can speak Japanese, call 110 for the police and 119 for an ambulance or fire department. If you don't know Japanese, ask someone who does to call.

6 Earthquakes are common in Japan. Most are small. If you're staying in a hotel, look for the earthquake instructions. Many modern buildings are built to sway with the earthquake and minimize damage. Just hold on and ride it out!

The United States Compared to Japan

	United States of America (USA)	Nippon koku
Official Name	United States of America (USA)	Nippon koku
Official Language	No official language, though English is most commonly used	Japanese
Population	325 million	127 million
Common Words	yes, no, excuse me	*hai* (hye), *lie* (ee-yeh), *sumimasen* (soo-mee-mah-sen)
Flag		
Money	Dollar	Yen
Location	North America	East Asia
Highest Point	Denali (Mount McKinley)	Mount Fuji
Lowest Point	Death Valley	Hachiro-gata
Size	World's third-largest country	About the size of California
National Anthem	"The Star-Spangled Banner"	"Kimigayo"

So now you know some important and fascinating things about my country, Japan. I hope to see you someday whizzing around on our bullet train, relaxing in one of our steamy hot springs, or visiting one of our many shrines. Until then . . . *sayonara*! Good-bye!

Glossary

ancestors (AN-ses-turz)
members of a family who lived long ago

annual (AN-yoo-uhl)
happening once every year

conserve (kuhn-SURV)
to use carefully to avoid loss or waste

emperor (EM-pur-ur)
the ruler of an empire

essentials (i-SEN-shuhlz)
items that are considered necessary and that one cannot do without

island (EYE-luhnd)
relating to a piece of land completely surrounded by water

kimonos (ki-MOH-nohz)
long, loose robes with wide sleeves and a sash

mascot (MAS-kaht)
an animal or symbol used to represent a group, place, or event that is supposed to bring good luck

shrines (SHRINEZ)
places that are considered holy where people go to worship

souvenirs (soo-vuh-NEERZ)
objects that a person keeps to remind him or her of a place or person or something that happened

sushi (SOO-shee)
a Japanese dish made with small cakes of cooked rice with raw fish or vegetables

traditions (truh-DISH-uhnz)
the customs, ideas, and beliefs that are handed down from one generation to the next

Index

Facts for Now

Visit this Scholastic website for more information on Japan and to download the Teaching Guide for this series:

www.factsfornow.scholastic.com   Enter the keyword **Japan**

About the Author

Wiley Blevins is an author living and working in New York City. His greatest love is traveling, and he has been to Japan many times. He loves taking photos while riding the bullet train— the trees and telephone poles look like they're bowing in the pictures. He has written numerous books for kids.